GW00546007

Tamara grew up in Coldstream, British Columbia, Canada, a beautiful suburb of a city nestled in the Okanagan Valley, where she grew up with two sisters on a ten-acre hobby farm, eventually going into healthcare, transcribing medical reports within her local hospital. Growing up, she saw herself as a shy, yet easily-made joyful child who was empathetically weighted. Empathy and intuition felt more of a burden than something to embrace and use and made her feel disconnected to a world she saw as hard, but her safety place was the same mind from which she tried to escape. Married at 21 and having three boys by 28, she felt the stretch into the light and dark of their extension as well. Writing became something she revisited from her youth. The poetic form it took became an inner language that through process helped to lift the weight, becoming her connection to soul and something greater, a sense of peace when acknowledging the human cry.

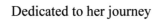

Dedicated to her journey

Tamara Hubacek

S.H.E.

A collection of expression

AUSTIN MACAULEY PUBLISHERS™

LONDON • CAMBRIDGE • NEW YORK • SHARJAH

A CIP catalogue record for this title is available from the British Library.

ISBN 9781528985956 (Paperback)
ISBN 9781528985963 (Hardback)
ISBN 9781528985970 (ePub e-book)

www.austinmacauley.com

First Published (2020)
Austin Macauley Publishers Ltd
25 Canada Square
Canary Wharf
London
E14 5LQ

She painted over pictures to say something more
She painted over what she was given before
She made new colours from what had been there
She took what was left and what she could spare
She made light and dark from one shade of black
She used the paint she carried on her back.
She wasn't an artist and didn't have time
She painted herself in between all the lines
She put on a tag, saying the cost is free
I don't care if you like it
Don't care if you like me.

Yells from all corners, printed and sang
She heard still their echoes from the places she came
A bidding, an auction, of what she could buy
She laid down her script and there let it lie
She only had peace as her income
Something she'd spent on those in her kingdom.
Since that was something that only bought truth
She took back her script
And what was left of her youth.

She wore wings, not like how a bird flies
She wore wings, like a phoenix before it dies
She wore wings, not because she couldn't run
Because she first thought, she had none
Seeing her reflection
What was not bare
She finally saw how she'd gotten there.

When her feet were cold
When there was no hand to hold
When her voice was sold
When her story was left untold
When she broke the mould
She felt alone.

No one knows nothin' till knowing your own
No one knows knowing, till its truth is told
Knowing that's borrowed, but not fully known, is nothing a
knower has ever been shown
Knowing is tapping into what's always been
Knowing is letting the light come back in
Knowing that now can hold knowing unknown
Knowing that now holds a truth of its own
Knowing is something that can't be unknown
Knowing is something you know on your own.

The same tree
Seen from her bed
It changed like the seasons in her head
Green to red
Winter dread
Seen from many rooms
Seen changing into blooms
Seen needing light and rain
Seeing old is new again
Broken limbs from storms gone by
Changing wind's lullaby.

Shallow, hollow, don't fall in
The hole you see has always been
Where and when and how become
The veil it lifts
The total sum
The fall into
What you avoid
Is coming from the spirit fold

Bathe and fall in waves that see.
Yes, you'll fall and you will be
Okay
All in all and through it be
My own truth to comfort me.
Today
She can hear a voice so quiet
She can cut and sew and dye it
To fit
From pieces that fell off she can break in certain places
Bending at the fears she faces
Once the crack is had and stacked
You really never get her back
Growing in strengt' creates a callus
Glass houses never make a palace.

This isn't for me
It's not my place
Those aren't my words
I don't feel safe
Don't hide
Stay you say
This doesn't feel like play.

I brought my lunch
You stayed away
You told me I should come today
I don't have room
Right or wrong, good or bad
No more room
To be more sad
Every time I came in sight
Took faith in you I had to fight
So, in this home of many views
I only have so much room.

She held a wand
A heavy weight

Fearing the strength it would take
Choice defined and consequence
Holding on till making sense
It's impossible to make a call
We're not meant to know it all
Taking on the hand that's dealt
Even magic summons help.

From inside I watch and wait
Feeling which piece to take
Nothing fits so I will go
Tailoring a piece to sew
When it's right
I will know
Nothing fits, so I will go.

Keep the tribe
Hand in trench
It was then
I knew you when
Broken now and lost a wing
They have you in their spirit ring
Old is new and new is old
Nothing is as it's told.

Dead but alive
I rise
Up but down
I fall
Through and carry
Crash and take
I wonder what next I'll make.

Disrupting peace
Not my horn
My release
Lyrics warn
A band that plays inside my head

Lyrics of the songs you said
Take your noise on parade
I'm playing the music that I made.

Falling off
Castaways
Taking back the stolen days
Rewriting what was off
Shifting lenses
Old ones tossed
What was there need not be set
Seeing all in retrospect
Players, walkers, hopeless game
Honour in the walk and fame
I hope to gather at the end
Him and her, all of them
Gardens of lands of green
This is what I think I've seen.
Don't we all have this dream.

A shift, a mass, changing form
Taking all, whole and torn
Just let go and take the sail
Sometimes carried when we fail.
It will take your whole life to survive
You will give away the live in alive
Sometimes all you can do is drift
Knowing that it's more than this.

Light finds cracks and finds its route.

Every height casts shadows low
Places where the light won't show
Every corner and hidden hollow
Has taken cover where light can't follow
You shine your light to see your path
Yet darkness there, beyond the cast
Some will follow a lighted walk

Some are blinded and cannot
What connects me to you
Are the things we've all been through
Sometimes light is just a beam
That shows where we've already been
And you've been seen.

What many call weakness is actually strength
What many don't see is what all it takes
What many destroy never actually dies
Ashes with wind spread and rise
What many turn from is their own voice.
What they hate is having had the choice
We often breathe in someone's exhale.
Adding weakness to what was frail.
If your ship is sinking and you can't keep the weight
Remember what wasn't yours to take.

Her voice was her chords, her poetry lyrics
Her laughter rebellion of what they were selling
Her thoughts the next song for someone to sing
Water her muse
Because lakes come from springs
Words that flow like water to thirst
What ends begins with what starts first.

Raven, he watched from afar
He came and told of his battle scars
He found a way to laugh and live
Yet knew the little he could give
So Raven shared his strength and power
By telling his tales of flying miles
When the moon called for his final flight
He'd already had it in his sights
Raven's stories that made us laugh
Came from pain from the distance passed
Miles of flight
On wings to bear

Tales of hope that got him there.

Far like thunder, distant sky
Settling over, wondering why
All to come. All to feel
Something's brewing, my fate to seal
I will heal. I will heal
Yet in passing, in the midst
Remembering it's not all this.
.
It's taught, it's bought, it's talked about
I'm in doubt. I'm in doubt
This is not what I asked
I'll collect the rain while it lasts
And drink.

A bird called like any other
Yet somehow sounded like a brother
I couldn't see him
Now he's gone
Not before I heard his song
Maybe he sees me, maybe he knows
Maybe he told me beauty unfolds
Maybe he reminds me I'm not alone
Maybe he told me I'm always home
Maybe it really was just a bird
Maybe I heard a sacred word.

The witch you burned came back reborn
She knew nothing of hate
Nothing of scorn
She first forgot what had remained
But pain made her remember again
flee
She sees the pain you inflict on others
Feels it like she is their mother
A fire still burns.

But lights the way
Reminding her from where she came

I thought I could do it but ran out of steam
I thought I could do it but ran out of faith
I thought I could do it but got lost for words
So I cried
It echoed
She spoke in my tongues
She sang the songs I wrote and threw away
She taught using my lessons I thought were mistakes
I now use the echo to lead me back home
And now have a knowing that voice is my own.

I am my forever home
The rooms are many and not always just my own
Visitors connected through time and space
Come in and out and through this place
Its walls I painted and my art hung high
Because they aren't for every eye
The inn of me isn't always open
Some doors are shut and the windows broken
I lock the locks and shut the doors
But sometimes the tea I pour is yours.

Pitter patter, what's the matter?
This soul I carry, it's so big my hands so small
I just can't carry it all
It's okay, your soul, it knows
It has a way of taking form, lift the load
Sometimes carried, sometimes towed
But I see things I don't want to see
But I've got you and you've got me
But my feet are tired, such a way to go
There's no prize for finishing first
It's the journey that creates the thirst
You have to take care of that first
Your feet are small for a reason

For every stage, there is a season
It's your time to see your power
Watch it grow and watch it matter
Peace and stillness are top of list
Without them, the biggest pieces are missed
I am listening, but I'm not sure
It's not what it appears
Not what we're taught and worth our fears
The journey does not end here
You'll sing, dance and laugh and when you don't, you'll feel
CFFontrast
The heavy from which you learn to create, the opposite from
the things you hate
But I can't do that by myself
There's help out there and in your soul
Something that connects us all
But how do you know that it's true
Because you've got me and I've got you.

Tick, tock, watch the clock
Hurry or your momentum stops
Run. Run. You're behind
Hurry or yours will be mine
No, I'll stay
Stay a while and smell a rose
If you get it, it is yours
My journey is not a race
I can dance at any pace
What is meant for me will not pass
Water exists without a glass
I let the silence drown out the noise
If you get it, it is yours.

Forest lush and green
Hidden away
Mostly unseen
Take me away and make me lost
Lost in all that is you
Bathe me in your scent and sounds
I'll walk barefoot on your ground
You can remind me what it is
To be alive just like a kid.

Wisdom we bring with us gets forgotten
Unlike the wisdom from the systems we are taught in
Wisdom gained through life gets tainted
Not knowing if it was served or attraction awaited
Wisdom from age can bring regret
Connected by a thread we don't see yet.

The soul sees what the eyes cannot
The heart beats a drum from a distant land
It knows a rhythm not taught by man
The spirit heals what the body fights
The inner being turns on the lights
Voice meets ear which hears another
Who then in turn shares with another
One to one to others we share
Because we all have a cross to bear.

Your truth, it is not mine
This story, it goes back in time
Your fears just are not my own
I do not worry about coming home
That place I have already known.
I'm allowed to make mistakes
My soul it takes time
Past, present, future mine.

The wind comes strong
When already the nights are long
What else can one bear
Go inside and simplify
Warm the cockles of your mind
The work not mental but in spirit
I'm going in to feel it.

Circumstance is worldly
Something that need not destroy me
Earthly troubles have always been
Paralyzing gifts within
I gift myself a little peace
Its more than just survival
Relief.

Two steps forward then three back
Chaos breeds to manage that
One destroys what one creates
Thoughts to words to action makes
Giving power to what is not
Holding there, I forgot.

You do you and I do me
Destruction need not barrier be
To what comes forth from what I see
I see. I see
For every wrong there is a right.

It's not always in sight
The light
Working despite the other
Not bound by the work of another
Light shines despite being seen
When you can't stand
Lean.

It's the light that holds the power
Darkness comes every hour
Turning away doesn't keep you safe
You can't really leave this place
In the dark
If you have light
Let it burn
Let it burn till it's your turn
Go as far as the light will touch
Without the light
You can't do much.

You lack control, and so it is
It makes you feel just like a kid
You implode far too often
Who you were you have forgotten
Remember when a breeze brought relief
The sound of a fallen leaf
The laugh within
The world's caved in
A little scared.
Your safe is on trial
You've not felt peace in a while
Yet something of the lightness known
Images your soul was shown
Something there you knew was true
I remember you.

Take and break and merry make
All for self and others' sake
Using cloth from which you wove
Warming others at the close
Honouring the fabric threads
Making peace with what you dread.

I give to her my gifts and wisdom
I know she's here to live them
I leave for her what I know

I show her what I can show
Not because she's earned her worth
Rather, something bestowed at birth
I help her on the path to see
Because the one I guide is me.

I take what is not and bury it away
Just like a festering wound
It will grow. I'll see it soon
Left alone and sometimes forgotten
It lacking attention
With the ancient extension
The soil to take what's offered to be
Bringing essentials of lost history
Now extended through a thought come to be
Touched by me
While my focus turned and mind unaware
My offering was growing the leaves it now bears.

The past looked to future
The future to past
Not Knowing that now is all of that
Dust to dust, stirring spreads
Using new tools to make ancient bread.

Shards of glass falling fast
Breaking at the fall
Nothing heard in aftermath
Nothing heard at all.
Sound of breaking, hitting ground
Now not left with a sound
Any break that is to be
Triggers something known to me
I shake and take my walk the same
Same as others known by name.

While so big, so very small
One cannot hold it all

Through the breaks, the pieces fall
Leaving what you always knew
Full of breath and yet to breathe
Holding on until reprieve
Loudness when the wind it howls
A song it sings.
Carried for miles
Doors closed and windows tilted
To tame the breeze of lessons yielded.

Far like thunder, distant sky
Settling over, wondering why
All to come
All to feel
Shh, shh, it's okay my dear
Yes, something's brewing, fate to seal.

Oh yes, this is quite the ordeal
The rain soaks in
The wind will hiss
Try to remember it's not all this
What moves in will also pass
Enjoy the raindrops while they last.

Put it away like rot needs a seed.

The past looked to future
The future to past
Not knowing that now is all of that
Dust to dust
Unstillness to spread
Using new tools to make ancient bread.

She risked a lot
I'll make her proud
She got brave when life got loud
She ate the bread and kept her hair
What they said she didn't care

She said no and yes and stop
She let go of what she fought
She laughs and cries and lives and dies
She tries.

When every step felt like a mile
When a hit hurt a while
Washing away yet still more dirt
When even the wind it hurt
Lack and yet such overflow
There's much more you didn't know.

What was loud was not the sound
What was walked was not the ground
When she saw she wasn't seen
When she couldn't make a scream
She used what she could reach
And made a podium from which to teach
The height she found from what she climbed
Made her look back to that ground
Her boot is still in the mud still stuck
Left behind, more than luck
Something in the sand, so quick
She hadn't even noticed it
The
She may not be there anymore
She may have walked away
Her foot is still
Cold today
Climbing journeys feels alone
Out of sight and out of tone
But when your metal at the top
Falls to ground
You pick it up.